Library of Congress Control Number: 2014915172
ISBN: 978-1-4951-2517-1
© 2014 Medical Management International, Inc. (dba Banfield Pet Hospital®)

For permission requests, write to the publisher at the address below:

Banfield Pet Hospital
8000 NE Tillamook St.
Portland, OR 97213
Attn: Permissions Coordinator

Printed by our good friends at...

PREMIERPRESS.COM
Portland, Oregon

Dedicated to anyone who has
ever loved a pet.

I lose my chew toy
all the time.

Help me find it
on every page!

Hello reader!

Just like our pets, kids have very, very busy days too! We go to school, do our homework (my favorite subject is science), play with friends and hang out with family. Plus, we save time for some of our favorite hobbies like reading a good book, playing a sport or riding our bikes.

If you have a pet, you know they need lots of attention and love as well. My two dogs Sammie and Shuga are a lot of fun, but they can also be a lot of work. Whether it's feeding them, making sure they get enough exercise or taking them to the veterinarian for their preventive care, our pets rely on us to keep them healthy and happy.

My love of pets is one reason I am so excited to work in partnership with Banfield Pet Hospital on this special book. When I grow up, I want to be a veterinarian so I can help families take the best care of their pets. *My Very, Very Busy Day* gives us a peek into what pets do all day, and is a story about everything a pet needs to be healthy and happy. I hope you enjoy this book as much as I do!

And who knows, maybe someday I'll see you at the veterinarian's office when you bring your pet in for a visit with (the future) Dr. Quvenzhané Wallis!

Happy reading!

Quvenzhané Wallis

2013 ACADEMY AWARD®
Best Actress nominee and pet lover

Purrrrrrrrrr!

Wake up! Wake up!

It's time to wake up!

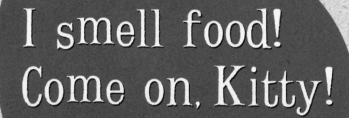

I smell food!
Come on, Kitty!

Kitty is my
best friend.

I am not.

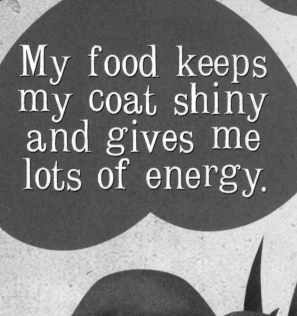

Playing makes me thirsty!

I love cool, fresh water.

I love my tongue.

Oh boy!
A car ride.

We're going to
the veterinarian.

Hairball
Heights

Rover Road

Paw Print Place

Woof Way

The vet is my doctor. She helps keep me healthy.

The vet
takes care
of all kinds
of pets.

I love my vet and she loves me!

Dr. Jessica Trice has been with Banfield for eight years and lives in Chicago. At home, you will find her reading with her cat Mariah and practicing martial arts. She has a black belt in Taekwondo and is a two-time grand champion of the US Open Taekwondo Championships. Dr. Trice is passionate about preventive care and volunteers by teaching children how to care for their pets at home.

Dr. Ari Zabell has been with Banfield for more than 18 years and lives in Vancouver, WA with his family and his two dogs, Jasmine and Elias. In his free time, Dr. Zabell loves to read, explore new places and foods, and build things around the house. He volunteers at preventive care clinics for pets belonging to the homeless.

Thank you to these Banfield Pet Hospital veterinarians for providing their medical expertise during the development of this book. To find the Banfield hospital nearest you, please visit Banfield.com.

My Best Friend Promise

Kids play a very important role in the family, especially when it comes to keeping pets happy and healthy. Make this promise as a way to remember how you can help your family take the very, very best care of your pet!*

I promise to:

- Feed my pet healthy food
- Give my pet fresh water every day
- Give my pet lots of exercise
- Keep an ID tag on my pet
- Be a safe pet owner and never leave my pet alone in a car
- Take my pet to the vet for regular check-ups
- Give my pet lots and lots and lots of love and kisses

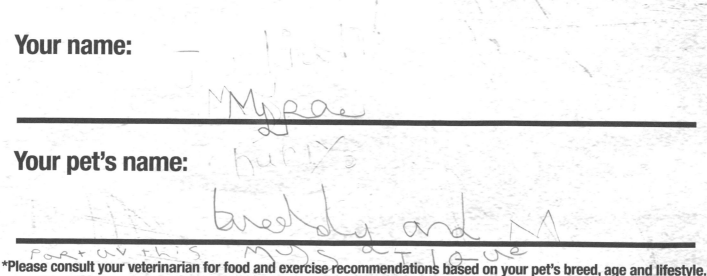

Your name:

Myrae

Your pet's name:

*Please consult your veterinarian for food and exercise recommendations based on your pet's breed, age and lifestyle.